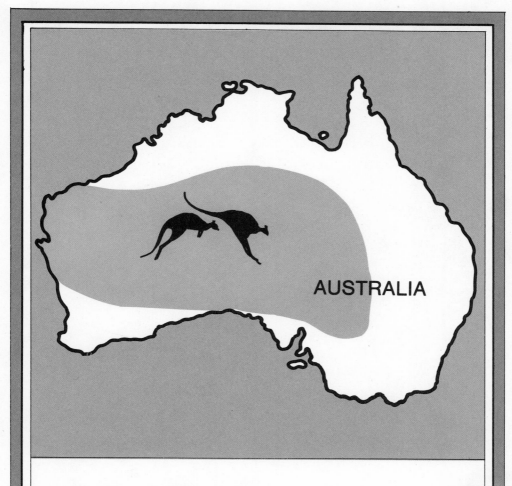

AUSTRALIA

There are two large groups of kangaroos, the reds and the grays. Most of them live in Australia. The red kangaroos live on the grassy plains shown on the map above.

Little Blue and Rusty
Red Kangaroos

By Sally Glendinning

GARRARD PUBLISHING COMPANY
CHAMPAIGN, ILLINOIS

Photo Credits

Toni Angermayer/National Audubon Society Collection/Photo Researchers: p. 21
Animals Animals/Douglass Baglin: p. 13
Animals Animals/Hans and Judy Beste: p. 9
Animals Animals/Ko jo Tanaka: p. 38
Australian Information Service: pp. 7, 11, 20, 34
Australian Tourist Commission: pp. 31, 32-33
Jen and Des Bartlett/National Audubon Society Collection/Photo Researchers: p. 18
John Dominis, Life Magazine, © Time, Inc.: pp. 2, 26, 29
Editorial Photocolor Archives: p. 5
C. B. and D. W. Frith/Bruce Coleman, Inc.: p. 8
George Holton/National Audubon Society Collection/Photo Researchers: p. 36
A. B. Joyce/National Audubon Society Collection/Photo Researchers: p. 23
Tom McHugh/National Audubon Society Collection/Photo Researchers: pp. 17, 40

**Cover art and map on page 1 by Benjamin C. Blake.
Art on page 15 by Arabelle Wheatley.**

Library of Congress Cataloging in Publication Data

Glendinning, Sally.
    Little Blue and Rusty.

    (Young animal adventures)
    SUMMARY: Describes a red kangaroo family in the
Australian grasslands, focusing on the first year of
the baby Rusty.
    1. Red kangaroo—Juvenile literature. [1. Red
kangaroo. 2. Kangaroos] I. Wheatley, Arabelle.
II. Title. III. Series.
QL737.M35G43   599.2   80-13935
ISBN 0-8116-7502-5

Little Blue and Rusty: Red Kangaroos

Big Red, a male red kangaroo, stood up and looked around. He was six feet tall when he stood up straight. He weighed nearly 200 pounds. The fur on his back was golden red in the sunlight. He was big and strong, with a broad chest, powerful legs, and a long tail. His big ears twitched to keep the flies away from his head. He held his head high as he looked about. He listened for any sound that might mean danger.

Big Red's mate was Blue Flyer. Like most female red kangaroos, her fur was soft blue-gray. She was less than five feet tall, and she had big eyes and a soft, pointed nose. There was a fur pouch across the lower part of her belly. She kept herself looking nice by combing her fur every day with her front claws and a special claw on each hind foot.

Blue Flyer's pouch was large now, for Little Blue was in it. Little Blue was eight months old, almost too big to fit into the pouch. Now she wanted to get out. Blue Flyer leaned over so the little one could jump out onto the grass.

This baby kangaroo, called a joey, is almost too big
to fit in its mother's pouch.

Little Blue's fur was lighter in color than
her mother's. Her fur would get darker as she
grew older. She was about the size of a little
lamb, and her legs were cream-colored. Now
she hopped around her mother, ready to play
games. Her favorite game was to bump into

her mother. Then Little Blue would run away before her mother could catch her.

But today, Little Blue ran too far. She bent down and ate some grass, then she hopped away to find some more.

Suddenly, she saw a big snake. It was coiled up on the grass not far away. The snake started to stretch its head toward Little Blue.

Kangaroos like to be with other kangaroos.
When a large group feeds and travels together,
it is called a mob.

The little kangaroo was frightened. She ran to her mother and jumped headfirst into her mother's pouch. Now Little Blue knew that she was safe.

Big Red and Blue Flyer hopped off to find green grass in a safer place. They hopped along slowly on all four feet.

It was early morning on the grassy plains of Australia, where the kangaroo family lived. The plains were bare except for a few trees and a bit of woodland here and there. The leaves on the trees were still green, but the grass was beginning to turn brown. No rain had fallen for many months.

Most of the time, the family traveled alone. Sometimes they met other kangaroos and stayed with them for a week or two. When they joined other kangaroos, they became part

10

of a mob. A big group of kangaroos has always been called a mob.

Big Red saw a water hole. The water shone like a mirror in the sun. Big Red could see that the grass around the water hole was fresh and green. He lifted his front paws and bounded toward the water hole. Blue Flyer and Little Blue followed. They hopped in giant leaps on their hind legs. They looked as if they were flying, for the toes on their hind feet hardly touched the ground.

Other kangaroos were resting under trees near the water hole. Big Red, Blue Flyer, and Little Blue joined the mob. They ate some grass and drank a little water. Then they lay down under a tree for a nap.

After a while Big Red got up and wandered off by himself. Male kangaroos like to be alone

Kangaroos hop along on their strong
back legs. They use their tails for balance.

This male kangaroo may use his short front legs to fight, but he also uses his strong back legs to kick the other male.

sometimes. Blue Flyer and Little Blue stayed under the big, shady tree. Another male kangaroo hopped over and sat down beside Blue Flyer. He wanted Blue Flyer for his mate.

Big Red saw the other male sitting by Blue Flyer. He roared in anger. He scratched his chest with his front paws and roared again. The other male stood up and moved toward Big Red. The two males would fight for Blue Flyer.

Big Red caught the other kangaroo by the shoulders. The other kangaroo caught Big Red. Both of the big males held their heads back. They moved about on their hind legs, clawed each other, and growled.

Big Red stood as tall as he could. He balanced for a moment on his tail. Then he

14

swung his hind legs forward and hit the other
kangaroo on the chest. The other kangaroo fell
backward. He lay on the grass for a moment.
Then he got up slowly and tried to fight again.
But he could not hurt Big Red. At last the
other kangaroo gave up and hopped away.

Blue Flyer would be Big Red's mate until another male who was a better fighter came along.

Big Red gave another little growl and sat down beside Blue Flyer. She was combing the dust from her fur as if nothing had happened. Then she licked and combed Little Blue's fur.

Little Blue tried to climb inside her mother's pouch. Blue Flyer pushed her away. Little Blue tried once more. This time Blue Flyer gave her a harder push. Then Little Blue put her head inside Blue Flyer's pouch. She drank some milk from the nipple that had fed her since she was born. Blue Flyer held her gently by the shoulders so she could not get into the pouch.

Now Little Blue knew she was on her own. She would be able to drink milk until she was

16   This joey has put its head inside its mother's pouch
to drink some of her rich milk.

a year old. But she was too big to ride in the pouch.

The next day, Blue Flyer sat with her back against the trunk of a tree. She licked the inside of her pouch until it was very clean. She was getting the pouch ready for a new

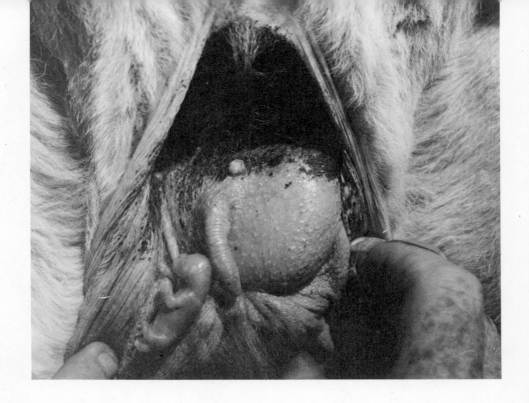

baby. Female red kangaroos usually have a new baby every eight months.

Rusty was born the next day. He didn't look like a kangaroo. He was about the size and shape of a pink jelly bean, and he weighed less than one ounce. Only his front feet with their tiny claws were ready to use when he was born.

The mother kangaroo's pouch is pulled back to show the new baby who is nursing. The nipple to the right of the baby will still be used by the joey who has left the pouch.

Now it was Rusty's turn to ride in Blue Flyer's pouch. But first he had to get there by himself. Blue Flyer might hurt him if she tried to help, for he had no fur at all to cover his little body.

Rusty used the claws on his front feet to climb the few inches from the birth opening to the pouch. Slowly he pulled himself up through Blue Flyer's fur until he reached the pouch. Then he crawled inside. His tiny mouth was wide open when he found the nipple that would feed him. He put his mouth tightly against it and started to drink the milk.

Now Blue Flyer's body began to make two kinds of milk. The milk from the nipple that fed Little Blue was rich and creamy. The milk for Rusty was like skim milk. It was just right for the new baby.

19

The kangaroos stayed near the water hole
until they had eaten almost all the grass.
Then Big Red and Blue Flyer knew that it
was time to move on. They hopped off one
night with Little Blue beside them. Rusty was
in Blue Flyer's pouch. By morning, they were
in a new field a long way from the water hole.

During the weeks that followed, the days became warmer. The air was still and quiet, except for the buzzing of flies. The hot sun burned the grass until it became too dry to eat. The kangaroo family rested most of the day. After the sun went down, they hopped

about looking for grass. If they could find green grass, they would not need much water.

Inside the pouch, Rusty was growing bigger and stronger. His eyes opened, and fur began to grow on his plump little body. His hind legs and his tail grew longer. Now Blue Flyer put her head inside the pouch each day. She licked the baby's fur and made soft little sounds to him.

Rusty was four months old when he first looked out of the pouch. That was the day the kangaroo family hopped past a farmer's cottage. Next to the cottage was a garden the farmer's wife had planted. There was a fence around the garden to keep out animals.

All the plants were fresh and green. The farmer's wife had saved rainwater in a big tank so she could water the garden during the

dry weather. The garden vegetables would feed her family.

Big Red stopped to look at the green plants, for he was hungry. He gave a leap and jumped over the fence. Then Blue Flyer jumped over the fence, too. Rusty looked out from the pouch to see where they were going. Little

Blue knew she couldn't jump over the fence, so she went through a hole under the fence.

Big Red, Blue Flyer, and Little Blue nibbled the green leaves on the plants. The kangaroo family was hungry, and the fresh green leaves tasted very good.

It was not long before the farmer's wife looked out the kitchen window. She saw the kangaroos in her garden. She was very angry. She ran outside with a broom in her hand. Quickly, she opened the gate to the garden and tried to make the kangaroos leave. The kangaroos were frightened. Big Red hopped close to the farmer's wife. Then he gave a mighty leap and jumped over her and the fence at the same time. The woman was so surprised that she dropped her broom.

Blue Flyer and Little Blue were too

frightened to go near the farmer's wife and through the gate. So Blue Flyer waited until Little Blue went back through the hole under the fence.

When Little Blue was safe, it was Blue Flyer's turn to jump to safety. The farmer's wife had picked up her broom and was waving it at Blue Flyer. Blue Flyer gave a mighty leap. But she was so frightened that she did not jump high enough.

Blue Flyer cut her broad tail on the sharp fence. She was in pain as she hopped slowly away.

It would be many days before the cut on Blue Flyer's tail was healed. Until then, she would not be able to hop very well nor jump very far.

After that, the days became even hotter.

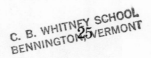

Now there were a few clouds in the sky, but still no rain fell. Big Red led his family across the plains looking for food and water. Sometimes he stopped to sniff the air for the smell of rain. But there was no rain. The hot wind kept on blowing dust and dead grass through the air.

Rusty left Blue Flyer's pouch for the first time when he was six months old. The kangaroo family had stopped to rest. Rusty poked his head out of the pouch and then tumbled down onto the brown grass. When he tried to get up, his little legs wobbled.

After that, Rusty climbed out of the pouch for a little while each day. Blue Flyer watched him carefully. She knew that this was the most dangerous time for a little kangaroo. A big lizard might come out of a hole and eat him. A snake might bite him. And there were other dangers, too.

One day Rusty climbed out of the pouch and looked around. He hopped a few steps toward Little Blue, hoping she would play with him. Instead, Little Blue hopped quickly toward her mother.

This joey is learning to stand on his own feet. Notice how big they are!

Suddenly Rusty saw a big bird in the sky. He was afraid. He hid under a bush and stayed there, shaking with fear.

In seconds, a great wedge-tailed eagle dived to the spot where Rusty had stood. The eagle was looking for a meal for its young. The eagle flew up to a branch. It sat there, waiting for Rusty to come out from under the bush.

The wedge-tailed eagle, left, is looking
for something to eat. In the picture below,
the joey is riding upside down
in its mother's pouch.

Blue Flyer hopped toward the bush. Just as
Rusty came out and leaped into her pouch, the
eagle flew close to Blue Flyer's head. Rusty
was safe, but he was still frightened.

One day Big Red smelled rain in the air from the north. The kangaroo family moved that way. As they were passing some gum trees, Big Red stopped. He hopped over to a tree and leaned against it to scratch his back. He moved his back from side to side against the trunk of the tree.

Something high in the tree growled and growled again. It was a loud, fierce growl. The kangaroos were afraid, for any loud noise frightened them.

Big Red bounded away from the tree. Rusty fell headfirst into his mother's pouch. Blue Flyer hopped after Big Red, with Little Blue by her side.

When they were safely away from the tree, the kangaroos turned and looked back. Now they were curious about what had made the

noise. They hopped back to see. On one of the
branches sat a koala with her baby on her
back. The koala looked like an angry teddy
bear. She growled again, and the baby koala
screamed. The koala did not often make noise,
but she was angry with Big Red. He had
shaken the gum tree when he scratched his

31

back against it. The gum tree was her home, and the gum tree leaves were the food she liked best to eat.

The kangaroos hopped away, following the smell of rain. Big, black clouds filled the sky above them. They were tired now, and hungry.

The kangaroos came to a bit of woodland. A small creek flowed through it. After the kangaroos drank some water, they sat on the brown grass to rest.

Big Red's ears began to twitch. He moved his head from side to side. He stood up

straight and tall. Then he thumped the ground
with his hind feet. That meant "Danger!"

Four hungry dingoes came out from the
bushes that grew on the banks of the creek.
They were fierce wild dogs with yellowish fur
and wolflike faces. One dingo tried to catch
Blue Flyer, who could not yet leap very fast.
Her tail was still sore. She leaned forward,

34

Australian dingoes are wild dogs.
This mother and puppy are coming
out of the bushes.

trying to leap faster. Rusty fell out of her
pouch near an old log on the ground. He
stayed there without moving.

Little Blue hopped from side to side. One
dingo tried to catch her. Then he joined the
other three, and they ran toward Big Red.

Big Red stood on his hind legs as the hungry
dingoes came toward him. Growling fiercely,
they attacked Big Red from all sides. One
dingo caught Big Red's tail in his mouth. Big
Red picked up that dingo in his front paws
and killed it. The other dingoes bit Big Red
and hurt him, but he killed them all. Then he
hopped back to Blue Flyer.

She made sad sounds as she hopped about
looking for Rusty. When he heard her, Rusty
cried softly. He hopped over to his mother and
got into her pouch. Little Blue came from

behind a bush, and the family was together once again.

They stayed together in the woodland. Other kangaroos came there, too. They came in family groups, the young ones near their mothers. The big males led the way. Now, once again, Big Red and his family were part of a mob of kangaroos.

The kangaroos were too tired and hungry to travel, so they sat quietly under the trees. Some of them would die soon unless they could find something to eat.

More dark clouds moved overhead. A few drops of rain started to fall. More and more raindrops came down. It rained for three days and three nights. Water filled the little creek until it flowed like a river. Rain soaked the ground. Green grass once more began to grow.

Blue Flyer and Little Blue went to stand in the creek. The cool water felt good. The other kangaroos began to move about. They hopped this way and that, eating the new grass.

Soon Little Blue and the other young kangaroos began to play games. They raced each other as they hopped about. Rusty played the same game Little Blue had played when

These wallabies, relatives of the red kangaroos, play and feed as the grass gets greener.

she was his age. He hopped close to Blue Flyer
and bumped into her. Then he hopped away
before she could catch him.

The kangaroos became fat and strong.
Before long, Little Blue would be as big as her
mother. Little Blue would start a family of

her own when she was about two years of age.

Rusty was growing up, too. His tan fur was beginning to turn red. In another year or two, Rusty would look just like his father. In no time, Rusty would be too big to get into his mother's pouch. Blue Flyer would push him away, for it would be time for a new baby to crawl into the pouch.

The mob of kangaroos moved across the plain, eating grass. Big Red stopped to look and listen for danger. His fur shone in the sun.

A flock of birds flew past him. The sound of their wings flapping sent Big Red bounding off in great leaps. The others followed him. Their tails were stretched out, and their strong hind legs pushed them faster and faster across the plains. Now there was grass enough to feed them for a long, long time.

Index